JERUSALEM TRAVEL GUIDE

From Ancient History to Modern Marvels: Your Ultimate Guide to Jerusalem

By

Williams Ritz

Table of Contents

Chapter One

Introduction to Jerusalem

Jerusalem is a city that has captivated the hearts and minds of people all around the world for thousands of years. Situated at the crossroads of three continents, it has been a hub of trade, religion, and culture since ancient times. Its significance to various religions and cultures is unparalleled, making it one of the most revered and contested cities in the world.

Jerusalem's history dates back to the Bronze Age, when it was a small

Canaanite city called "Urusalim." Over the centuries, it was ruled by the Egyptians, Babylonians, Persians, Greeks, Romans, Byzantines, Arabs, Crusaders, Ottomans, British, and eventually, the Israelis. Each conqueror left their mark on the city, resulting in a rich and diverse history that can still be seen and felt today.

Jerusalem's significance to Judaism is rooted in the city's association with King David, who made it the capital of his kingdom over 3,000 years ago. It was also the site of the First and Second Temples, which were the holiest sites in Judaism until they were destroyed by the Babylonians and Romans, respectively. Today, the Western Wall, the only remaining part of the Second Temple, is one of the most sacred places in Judaism and a symbol of Jewish resilience and faith.

For Christians, Jerusalem is the city where Jesus was crucified and resurrected, making it one of the holiest places in Christianity. The Church of the Holy Sepulchre, located in the Old City, is believed to be the site of Jesus' crucifixion, burial, and resurrection. It is a place of pilgrimage for Christians from all over the world and a testament to the enduring power of Jesus' message.

Islam also has a deep connection to Jerusalem, which is the third holiest city in Islam after Mecca and Medina.

According to Islamic tradition, the Prophet Muhammad ascended to heaven from the site of the Dome of the Rock, which is located on the Temple Mount. The Al-Aqsa Mosque, also located on the Temple Mount, is one of the most important mosques in the world and a symbol of the enduring presence of Islam in Jerusalem.

Beyond its religious significance, Jerusalem is a city of remarkable beauty and cultural richness. Its Old City, with its ancient walls, narrow streets, and historic landmarks, is a UNESCO World Heritage Site and a testament to the city's enduring legacy. The modern city, with its vibrant arts scene, diverse population, and bustling markets, is a testament to Jerusalem's continued vitality and relevance in the modern world.

In this guide, we will explore the many facets of Jerusalem, from its ancient history to its modern marvels. We will delve into the city's religious significance, its archaeological treasures, its museums and cultural landmarks, and its diverse cuisine and cultural traditions. Whether you are a history buff, a spiritual seeker, or simply a curious traveler, Jerusalem is a city that is sure to captivate your heart and mind.

Chapter Two

Exploring the Old City Jerusalem

The Old City of Jerusalem is one of the most fascinating and enchanting places on earth. With its labyrinthine streets, ancient walls, and iconic landmarks, it is a testament to the enduring legacy of this ancient city. The Old City is divided into four quarters, each with its own unique character and history: the Jewish Quarter, the Christian Quarter, the Muslim Quarter, and the Armenian Quarter. Each quarter is home to a wealth of historic sites, including the

Western Wall, the Church of the Holy Sepulchre, and the Dome of the Rock.

The Western Wall, also known as the Wailing Wall, is one of the most sacred sites in Judaism. Located in the Jewish Quarter, it is the last remaining remnant of the Second Temple, which was destroyed by the Romans in 70 CE. For Jews around the world, the Western Wall is a symbol of Jewish history, faith, and resilience. Visitors can write prayers and wishes on small pieces of paper, which they then place between the stones of the wall.

The Church of the Holy Sepulchre, located in the Christian Quarter, is one of the most important pilgrimage sites in Christianity. Built on the site where Jesus is believed to have been crucified, buried, and resurrected, it is a complex of churches, chapels, and shrines that have been built and rebuilt over the centuries. It is a testament to the enduring power of the Christian faith and a reminder of the complex history of Jerusalem.

The Dome of the Rock, located on the Temple Mount in the Muslim Quarter, is one of the most iconic landmarks in Jerusalem. Built in the 7th century, it is one of the oldest surviving Islamic structures in the world. It is believed to be the site where the Prophet Muhammad ascended to heaven, and it remains one of the most sacred places in

Islam. The dome is covered in gold leaf, which glimmers in the sunlight and can be seen from all over the city.

Beyond these iconic sites, the Old City is also home to a wealth of other historic landmarks, including the Tower of David, the Via Dolorosa, and the Austrian Hospice. The Tower of David, located in the Armenian Quarter, is an ancient citadel that has been fortified over the centuries. Today, it is home to a museum that explores the history of Jerusalem from ancient times to the present day. The Via Dolorosa, located in the Christian Quarter, is the route that Jesus is believed to have taken on the way to his crucifixion. It is marked by a series of 14 stations of the cross, each of which is a place of prayer and contemplation. The Austrian Hospice, located in the Muslim Quarter, is a beautiful building that dates back to the 19th century. It is a testament to the enduring presence of Christian communities in Jerusalem and a reminder of the complex history of this ancient city.

Visiting the Old City of Jerusalem is a once-in-a-lifetime experience that will stay with you forever. The sights, sounds, and smells of this ancient city are unforgettable, and the history and spirituality of the place are palpable. Whether you are a history buff, a spiritual seeker, or simply a curious traveler, the Old City is a place that you cannot afford to miss.

Chapter Three

Religious Sites in Jerusalem

Jerusalem is one of the most religiously significant cities in the world. It is home to some of the most important holy sites in Judaism, Christianity, and Islam, making it a sacred destination for millions of people from around the globe. Each of these religions has its own distinct history and traditions in the city, and their holy sites are a testament to their enduring legacy.

Judaism has a long and complex history in Jerusalem, dating back thousands of years. For Jews, the city is the spiritual center of the world, and it is home to many of the religion's most important sites. The most sacred site in Judaism is the Temple Mount, which is believed to be the site of the First and Second Temples. Today, the Temple Mount is home to two of the most iconic landmarks in the city: the Dome of the Rock and the Al-Aqsa Mosque. For Jews, the Western Wall is also a site of great importance. It is the last remaining remnant of the Second Temple, and it is a place of prayer, pilgrimage, and reflection for Jews from all over the world.

Christianity also has a long and complex history in Jerusalem. It is believed that

Jesus spent much of his life in the city, and it is home to many of the most important sites in the Christian faith. The most sacred site in Christianity is the Church of the Holy Sepulchre, which is located in the Christian Quarter of the Old City. It is believed to be the site where Jesus was crucified, buried, and resurrected. The Via Dolorosa, which is the route that Jesus is believed to have taken on the way to his crucifixion, is also a site of great importance for Christians. It is marked by a series of 14 stations of the cross, each of which is a place of prayer and contemplation.

Islam also has a deep and rich history in Jerusalem. It is believed that the

Prophet Muhammad ascended to heaven from the site where the Dome of the Rock is now located, making it one of the most sacred sites in Islam. The Al-Aqsa Mosque, which is also located on the Temple Mount, is one of the oldest mosques in the world and is also of great importance to Muslims.

Beyond these iconic landmarks, there are many other religious sites in Jerusalem that are of great significance to their respective religions. The Tomb of King David, located on Mount Zion, is a site of great importance for Jews, as it is believed to be the burial place of King David. The Garden Tomb, located just outside the walls of the Old City, is a site of great importance for Christians, as it is believed to be the site of Jesus' burial and resurrection.

Visiting these religious sites in Jerusalem is an experience that is both humbling and awe-inspiring. Whether you are a believer or not, the spirituality and history of these sites are palpable, and they offer a unique insight into the complex and rich tapestry of Jerusalem's religious history.

Chapter Four

Archaeology in Jerusalem

Jerusalem is a city steeped in history, and its many archaeological discoveries offer a unique glimpse into its rich and complex past. Archaeologists have been working in Jerusalem for over a century, unearthing countless artifacts and discoveries that have helped piece together the city's fascinating history.

One of the most significant archaeological sites in Jerusalem is the City of David. This ancient settlement dates back to the 4th millennium BCE and is believed to be the original location of Jerusalem before the city expanded to the north. The City of David has yielded many important discoveries over the years, including the Pool of Siloam, which is believed to be the site where Jesus healed a blind man in the New Testament.

Another significant archaeological site in Jerusalem is the Temple Mount, which is home to the Dome of the Rock and the Al-Aqsa Mosque. Archaeologists have been working on the Temple Mount for decades, uncovering many important discoveries that shed light on the history of the site. In recent years, archaeologists have used advanced technology to explore the site further, including ground-penetrating radar, which has revealed new information about the layout of the original temple.

Throughout the city, there are also many underground tunnels that have been discovered over the years. These tunnels date back to different periods in Jerusalem's history, and they offer a unique insight into the city's complex and layered past. Some of the most significant tunnels include the Western Wall Tunnels, which run underneath the Western Wall, and the Hezekiah Tunnel, which is an ancient water tunnel that dates back to the 8th century BCE.

The archaeological discoveries in Jerusalem are not just significant for historians and archaeologists; they also have a profound impact on the city's residents and visitors. They offer a tangible link to the past, and they help to preserve and protect Jerusalem's cultural heritage for future generations. The ongoing work of archaeologists in Jerusalem is critical in helping us to better understand the city's past, present, and future, and it is a testament to the enduring importance of this remarkable city.

Chapter Five

Jerusalem Museums and Artifacts

Jerusalem is a city that is rich in history and culture, and one of the best ways to explore its past is by visiting its many museums. From ancient artifacts to contemporary art, Jerusalem's museums offer visitors a chance to explore the city's diverse cultural heritage and its many contributions to the world.

The Israel Museum is one of the city's most well-known museums, and it is home to an extensive collection of artifacts and artworks that date back to ancient times. The museum is divided into several wings, including the Archaeology Wing, which features artifacts from the First Temple period to the Islamic conquest, and the Jewish Art and Life Wing, which showcases Jewish art and culture from around the world.

Another must-visit museum in Jerusalem is the Yad Vashem Holocaust Museum. This museum is dedicated to preserving the memory of the Holocaust and honoring its victims. The museum's exhibits include personal artifacts, photographs, and films that tell the stories of the millions of people who were affected by the Holocaust. The museum also features an extensive research center and library that is open to scholars and researchers.

The Museum of Islamic Art is another significant museum in Jerusalem, and it houses an impressive collection of Islamic art and artifacts from around the world. The museum's exhibits include calligraphy, ceramics, textiles, and other decorative arts, and they offer visitors a unique glimpse into the rich and diverse history of the Islamic world.

In addition to these museums, there are many other smaller museums and galleries throughout Jerusalem that are well worth a visit. These include the Tower of David Museum, which explores the history of the city's fortifications, the Bible Lands Museum, which features artifacts from the ancient

Near East, and the Bloomfield Science Museum, which offers hands-on exhibits and interactive displays on science and technology.

Overall, the museums and artifacts in Jerusalem offer a fascinating and comprehensive look at the city's cultural heritage and its many contributions to the world. Whether you are interested in ancient history, contemporary art, or the Holocaust, there is something for everyone in Jerusalem's many museums and galleries.

Chapter Six

The diverse culinary scene in Jerusalem

Jerusalem is a city that is known for its rich cultural heritage, and its food scene is no exception. The city's cuisine is a reflection of its diverse population, with influences from Jewish, Arab, and Mediterranean cultures. From traditional dishes to modern fusion cuisine, Jerusalem offers a wide range of culinary experiences for visitors to explore.

One of the best ways to experience Jerusalem's food scene is by visiting its famous markets. The Mahane Yehuda Market is one of the city's most popular markets, and it is home to an incredible array of fresh produce, spices, meats, and baked goods. The market also has many small cafes and restaurants that offer traditional Israeli and Middle Eastern dishes, such as hummus, falafel, and shakshuka.

Another popular market in Jerusalem is the Old City's Muslim Quarter, which is famous for its street food. Here, visitors can try traditional Palestinian dishes such as musakhan, which is roasted chicken with onions and sumac, and a sweet pastry made with cheese and syrup.

In addition to traditional dishes, Jerusalem also has a vibrant modern food scene. The city is home to many innovative restaurants and cafes that offer a fusion of different culinary styles. Some of the most popular modern restaurants in Jerusalem include Machneyuda, which serves modern Israeli cuisine, and Azura, which is famous for its Iraqi Jewish dishes.

For those looking to explore the city's wine scene, Jerusalem is also home to several wineries and tasting rooms. The city's wineries produce a wide range of wines, including traditional Israeli varietals like Cabernet Sauvignon and Merlot, as well as unique blends that incorporate local ingredients such as pomegranate and fig.

Overall, Jerusalem's food and drink scene offers a fascinating and delicious glimpse into the city's cultural heritage and its modern culinary innovations. Whether you are looking to explore the city's traditional dishes, its modern fusion cuisine, or its wine scene, Jerusalem has something for everyone to enjoy.

Chapter Seven

Overview of Modern Jerusalem

Jerusalem is a city that is steeped in history and tradition, but it is also a modern and vibrant metropolis with a diverse population and a thriving culture. In recent years, the city has undergone significant development, with new neighborhoods, shopping centers, and cultural institutions sprouting up alongside its ancient landmarks.

One of the most notable modern developments in Jerusalem is the

Mamilla Mall. This open-air shopping center is located just outside the walls of the Old City, and it features a wide range of high-end fashion boutiques, restaurants, and cafes. The mall's sleek, modern design is a stark contrast to the ancient stone walls of the Old City, and it has become a popular destination for tourists and locals alike.

Another modern landmark in Jerusalem is the Mahane Yehuda Market. This bustling marketplace has been a fixture in the city for over a century, but in recent years, it has undergone a significant transformation. Today, the market is home to many trendy restaurants, cafes, and bars, and it has become a hub for Jerusalem's young and hip residents.

In addition to its modern landmarks, Jerusalem is also home to a thriving cultural scene. The city is home to many theaters, galleries, and performance spaces, and it hosts several festivals throughout the year that celebrate everything from jazz music to street art. The Jerusalem Theater is one of the city's most well-known cultural institutions, and it hosts a wide range of performances, including theater, dance, and music.

Jerusalem's population is also incredibly diverse, with Jews, Muslims, Christians, and other religious and ethnic groups all living together in the city. This diversity is reflected in the city's cuisine, music, and art, and it has helped to create a vibrant and dynamic culture.

Generally, modern Jerusalem offers a fascinating contrast to its ancient past, with sleek new shopping centers and cultural institutions sitting alongside the city's historic landmarks. Whether you are interested in exploring the city's contemporary art scene, trying its innovative cuisine, or simply soaking up its unique atmosphere, you're sure to get a lasting impression.

Chapter Eight

Day Trips from Jerusalem

Jerusalem is a city with a rich history and culture, but it also serves as a perfect base for exploring nearby destinations. From ancient historical sites to natural wonders, there are plenty of day trips that are easily accessible from Jerusalem.

One of the most popular day trips from Jerusalem is a visit to Bethlehem, the birthplace of Jesus. Located just a few miles south of Jerusalem, Bethlehem is home to many important Christian sites, including the Church of the Nativity, which is said to mark the spot where Jesus was born. Visitors can also explore the historic Old City, where they can wander through the narrow streets and soak up the city's unique atmosphere.

Another popular destination for day trips from Jerusalem is the Dead Sea, which is located just a short drive east of the city. The Dead Sea is known for its high salt content, which makes it a popular destination for those looking to experience its unique health benefits. Visitors can float in the salty water, cover themselves in the mineral-rich mud, and even visit nearby spas and resorts for a relaxing day of pampering.

For those interested in ancient history, a day trip to Masada is a must-see. This historic fortress is located atop a steep cliff overlooking the Dead Sea, and it is one of Israel's most famous landmarks. Visitors can take a cable car to the top of the cliff and explore the ruins of the fortress, which dates back to the first century AD. The site is also famous for its tragic history, as it was the site of a mass suicide by Jewish rebels who were besieged by Roman soldiers.

Another popular day trip from Jerusalem is a visit to the city of Hebron, which is located in the southern part of the West Bank. Hebron is an important religious site for both Jews and Muslims, and it is home to the Tomb of the Patriarchs, which is said to be the burial site of Abraham, Isaac, and Jacob. Visitors can also explore the historic Old City, which is home to many important religious and cultural sites.

Finally, for nature lovers, a day trip to Ein Gedi is a must-see. This oasis is located on the shores of the Dead Sea and is home to a variety of rare plant and animal species. Visitors can explore the park's many hiking trails, swim in the cool waters of the nearby springs, and even spot wildlife like ibexes and hyraxes.

Overall, there are plenty of day trips from Jerusalem that offer something for everyone, whether you are interested in history, culture, or natural wonders. With so many nearby destinations to explore, Jerusalem serves as the perfect base for a memorable and diverse vacation.

Chapter Nine

Nature and Parks

While Jerusalem is known for its rich history and culture, it is also surrounded by some of Israel's most stunning natural landscapes. From lush forests to desert oases, there are plenty of nature and park destinations to explore around Jerusalem.

One of the most popular natural destinations near Jerusalem is the Ein Gedi nature reserve, which is located on the shores of the Dead Sea. This lush oasis is home to a variety of plant and animal species, including ibexes, hyraxes, and even the occasional leopard. Visitors can hike the reserve's many trails, swim in the cool waters of the nearby springs, and relax in the shade of the park's many trees and palm groves.

Another popular natural destination near Jerusalem is the Jerusalem Forest, which covers over 6,000 acres of rolling hills and pine forests just outside the city. The forest is a popular destination for hiking, biking, and picnicking, and it is also home to a variety of wildlife, including deer, foxes, and even the occasional wild boar.

For bird lovers, the Hula Valley in northern Israel is a must-see destination. This vast wetland is home to over 500 species of birds, including rare and endangered species like the Syrian Serin and the White-throated Kingfisher. Visitors can explore the many trails and observation points throughout the valley, and even take a guided bird-watching tour for a chance to spot some of the valley's more elusive species.

Another natural destination near Jerusalem is the Timna Park, located in the southern part of Israel, just a few hours' drive from the city. This stunning park is home to a variety of geological wonders, including colorful rock formations, towering sandstone pillars, and even the world's oldest copper mines. Visitors can explore the park's many hiking trails, take a scenic drive through the park's winding roads, and even camp overnight in one of the park's designated camping areas.

Finally, for those looking for a more unique natural experience, a visit to the Ramon Crater is a must-see. Located in the heart of the Negev desert, the Ramon Crater is a vast natural formation that was created by millions of years of erosion. Visitors can explore the crater's many hiking trails, take a guided jeep tour of the surrounding desert, and even stargaze under the clear desert sky.

Basically, there are plenty of nature and park destinations to explore around Jerusalem, each offering a unique and memorable experience for visitors of all ages and interests. Whether you're interested in hiking, bird-watching, or simply getting a feel of the beauty of Israel's natural landscapes, there is something for everyone to enjoy in the area surrounding Jerusalem.

Chapter Ten

Practical Information for Travelers

Visiting Jerusalem can be an unforgettable experience, but it is important to be prepared for the practicalities of traveling in the city. Here is a guide to the essential practical information you need to know before visiting Jerusalem:

Transportation:
Jerusalem is a city with an extensive public transportation system, which

includes buses, light rail, and taxis. Buses are the most common form of transportation in the city, with several bus companies operating routes throughout the city and beyond. The light rail system is another popular option, offering fast and efficient service between the central bus station and key locations in the city center.

Taxis are also widely available, but it's important to note that they can be expensive, especially for longer trips. To save money, consider sharing a taxi with other travelers or using a ride-sharing service like Uber or Gett.

Accommodations:

Jerusalem has a wide range of accommodations to suit every budget and preference, from luxury hotels to hostels and guesthouses. Some of the most popular areas to stay in Jerusalem include the Old City, the City Center, and the German Colony.

When choosing accommodations, it's important to keep in mind that some areas may be more conservative than others. In ultra-Orthodox neighborhoods, for example, it may be more appropriate to dress modestly and avoid public displays of affection.

Safety:

While Jerusalem is generally a safe city for visitors, it's important to take precautions to ensure your safety. One of the most important things to keep in mind is the ongoing conflict in the region, which can occasionally lead to violence and unrest. It's a good idea to stay up-to-date on current events and avoid any areas that may be considered high-risk.

It's also important to take basic safety precautions, such as staying aware of your surroundings, not flashing valuables in public, and avoiding walking alone at night, especially in isolated areas.

Cultural customs:

Jerusalem is a diverse and multicultural city, with a rich history and many different traditions and customs. When visiting, it's important to be respectful of the local customs and traditions, especially when visiting religious sites or interacting with members of different communities.

Some of the most important cultural customs to keep in mind include dressing modestly when visiting religious sites, avoiding public displays of affection, and being mindful of local customs around food and drink.

In conclusion, visiting Jerusalem can be a rich and rewarding experience, but it's important to be prepared for the practicalities of traveling in the city. By following these essential tips on transportation, accommodations, safety, and cultural customs, you can ensure that your visit to Jerusalem is safe, enjoyable, and respectful of local traditions and customs.

Conclusion

This guide has provided a comprehensive overview of Jerusalem, from its ancient history to its modern marvels. It has highlighted the many religious sites, museums, archaeological discoveries, and natural wonders that make Jerusalem a unique and fascinating destination for travelers from all over the world.

Visiting Jerusalem is an experience like no other. The city's rich history and cultural diversity offer endless opportunities for exploration and discovery. From the winding streets of the Old City to the contemporary landmarks of modern Jerusalem, there is always something new to discover and experience.

One of the most notable aspects of Jerusalem is its religious significance. As the birthplace of three major religions, the city is home to many important religious sites that are of great significance to millions of people around the world. The Western Wall, the Church of the Holy Sepulchre, and the Dome of the Rock are just a few of the many destinations that make Jerusalem a pilgrimage site for many.

But Jerusalem is not just a city of the past. The city's modern developments, including its vibrant culinary scene, contemporary landmarks, and diverse cultural offerings, make it a dynamic and exciting destination for travelers of all ages.

While visiting Jerusalem requires some preparation and awareness of local customs and traditions, the effort is well worth it. The city's residents are welcoming and friendly, and the experiences to be had are truly unforgettable.

Of course, as with any travel destination, there are practical considerations to keep in mind. This guide has provided information on transportation, accommodations, safety, and cultural customs to help make your visit to Jerusalem as enjoyable and hassle-free as possible.

Ultimately, Jerusalem is a destination that offers something for everyone. Whether you are interested in history, culture, religion, nature, or simply the joys of travel, this city has it all. It is a destination that will leave an indelible impression on your heart and mind, and a place that you will want to visit time and time again.

So, as you plan your trip to Jerusalem, use this guide as a resource to help you make the most of your time in this incredible city. From the stunning Old City to the natural wonders of the surrounding areas, Jerusalem is a destination that will leave you feeling inspired, enlightened, and enriched.